CHAPTER 6. Brand Design & Optimization
CHAPTER 7. Website Setup & Funnel Upgrade
CHAPTER 8. Advertising & Design
CHAPTER 9. Launching & Promoting the Brand
CHAPTER 10. The Journey

AFTERTHOUGHT

Hola! My name is Simon Hawk and I am writing this from my office on the island of Puerto Rico.

My background is in Design for Apparel & Agriculture. I now specialize in Brand Optimization, Management Consulting & Artistic Direction.

Over the past decade, I have worked with 100's of clients on everything from CBD product packaging to real estate investment proposals & Permaculture design.

After working in NYC, LA and SF and finally moved to the Caribbean to live on the
island of Puerto Rico in 2013. I work remotely managing projects for my clients &
advising on international marketing campaigns.

These are my personal websites :
www.SimonHawk.co
www.SageDesignConsult.com
www.HouseofZenPR.com
www.Hempzaa.com
www.Exotikos.co

WHY DID I WRITE THIS BOOK ABOUT BRANDING?

After 15 years of working as a freelance graphic designer, I noticed a few patterns in common branding mistakes that were hurting my clients.

There are often misconceptions in understanding what branding is and why it is essential to starting a successful business.

It is easy to undervalue graphic art or creativity in businesses focused on sales or tech. The truth is, having a design strategy to develop a beautiful

HOW TO BUILD A STRONG & BEAUTIFUL BRAND

Creating Your Online Flow

- A GUIDEBOOK FOR LAUNCHING ONLINE BUSINESSES QUICKLY & EASILY -

By Simon Hawk

(A ROADMAP TO HELP YOU CRAFT YOUR IMAGE & DESIGN YOUR BRAND. QUICK TIPS & RESOURCES FROM AN EXPERIENCED CONSULTANT.)

By
Simon Hawk

- Introduction quote -
"A brand is a visual experience.
Great experiences sell more products.
Create a beautiful experience for your clients.
Build something you are proud of showing to customers.
Manifest success by visualizing, planning and focusing on growing your business online.
Read more books.
Grow like a tree.
You got this.
You can do it.
I got your back."

-Exito-

Index

INTRODUCTION - Simon Hawk Personal Intro

CHAPTER 1. Intro to Branding
CHAPTER 2. Building a Vehicle for Success
CHAPTER 3. Breakdown of Resources
CHAPTER 4. Planning the Work
CHAPTER 5. Project Management & Outsourcing

brand can greatly increase profits.

While it may appear as an optional expense, it is essential to success. The quality of your visual branding is how you are evaluated, it's that simple.
If your evaluation is high, the amount they are willing to pay, will be high.
I want to help you to raise your value!

WHO IS THIS BOOK FOR ?

This is not a book about pretty pictures to show you how awesome other people's work is. This book was designed to educate you on how you can build your own beautiful brand. This book is for new startups, serial entrepreneurs, beginners to eCommerce, newbies in marketing and people who seriously want to improve their online business.

It is also for people who have not started their online business yet and are seeking a guide on how to do so.

I designed this book to be full of

information that helps the reader to understand what branding is, why it is important and how to do it remotely.

It has more advice and resources than images, so prepare for a deep read into how to upgrade your designs and what to use to optimize your brand.

WHY WORK REMOTELY ?

When you work remotely you can choose your own adventure and setup an office anywhere you want.
The steps, tips, hints, guides, strategies, methods and checklists featured in this book will allow you to reduce the amount of time you spend working.
You can increase your profits and live the life of your dreams by setting up an online business that operates smoothly.

Below are a few picture of places I have worked on this book. Literally, on a boat and at an Airbnb in a rainforest. In this book I will teach you how to do it too!

BEGIN IMPROVING YOUR FINANCIAL FUTURE !

This book is about more than just a branding for dummies knockoff or a shortcut to better logo design.
It is a blueprint to build a vehicle for financial independence and a method for improving your existing business. You can design the life you want to lead by setting up an efficient system for making money online.

Building a beautiful brand will help you get there faster by creating a sexy system for your designs and content. If you have a high-quality brand with well thought out design and matching content, customers will be more likely to pay a premium.

In the following chapters I will show you the tools I use to generate money online easily and enjoyably.

- Freedom -

"WE ARE ALL CAPABLE OF CREATING A LIFE FREE FROM STRESS.

THE GOAL SHOULD BE TO CREATE A LIFESTYLE THAT ALLOWS YOU TO MAKE MONEY IN AN EFFORTLESS AND GRACEFUL WAY."

- SIMON HAWK -

CHAPTER 1

INTRO TO BRANDING

Branding is made up of all the promotions of a particular product or company. It utilizes a combination of marketing, design and copy to create a stylized appearance.

Branding's core fundamentals are : Developing an iconic logo and uniform appearance on all content distributed. This means that customers can remember the name, the graphics and the photos that represent a product. Why you should invest in your brand?

The answer is simple, it increases profits. A recognizable high-quality brand will yield more sales over a longer period, because people repeatedly buy from brands they know and trust.

THE PROBLEM WITH MOST BRANDS

One of the first elements of a brand

and the aspect most people recognize about a company is the logo. Most brands don't have a good logo.
Great branding often uses customized fonts to be more legible & memorable to viewers. Many brands fail to put emphasis on a custom font or even stick to a color palette.

A great brand uses multiple methods to display its message and create a voice for the company it represents. Most brands fail to establish a set style of imagery, a defined style of writing, or processes to create consistency.
I frequently see companies overcomplicating their brand or designs with too many different styles.

Some of the most successful brands have simple messages with basic shapes as their logos. Think of Audi!

GREAT BRANDING EXAMPLES

Beautiful branding is not always complex and is often quite simple.

Below are examples of the longest

standing brands and when their logos were designed.

Each one of these corporations has spent time and resources to develop a unique brand. Their designs are timeless and as you can see they are still identifiable in black and white.

BAD EXAMPLES OF BRANDING

When a brand doesn't look good it is a poor representation of the company or product and will require rebranding. Below are examples of brands that had to redesign their logo after several years because it was not successful.

Each one of these companies has spent has had to spend more money to develop a better logo. Their designs do not look good in black and white.

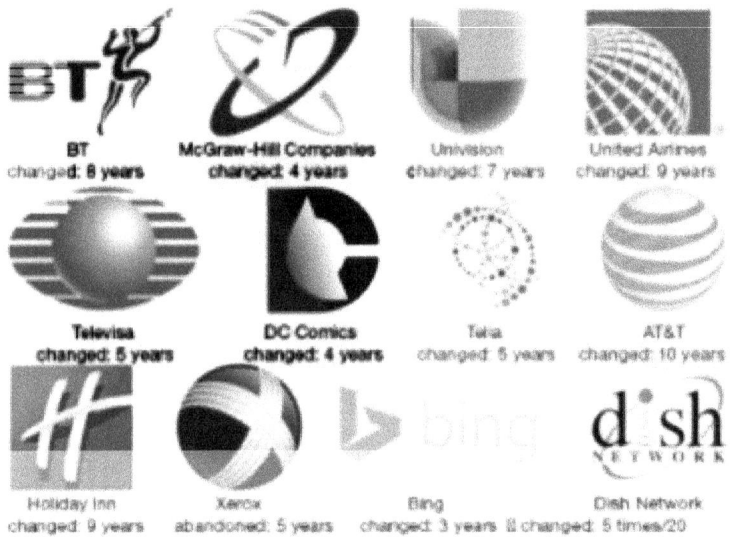

BETTER DESIGN = MORE SALES

In advertising they say,
"A picture is worth a thousand words."
If this is so, then a good design is
worth a thousand dollars in sales.

The perceived value of a product is directly related to the image or content that is presented to the consumer.

I often give the example to my graphic design clients that investing in Brand Design is like paying for clothing, you get what you pay for.

Good design is not always cheap, but it greatly improves the quality of the product.

With online sales, this is especially important as the customer cannot pick up the product and visuals are all we have to communicate.

A beautiful brand is the difference between a $50 price tag for a pair of generic sneakers and $500 for a trending designer or luxury fashion house.

The better the brand and the stronger the impact it has the more customers will remember it for its quality.

THE FORMULA FOR SUCCESS

Increasing the value of a product through better design & brandings seems simple, but people fail to put the pieces together.

I developed this equation after thinking about how to explain it best.

PV = (BP + MQ) x (VA + PC)

Product Value = (Brand Perception + Marketing Quality) x (Value Added + Product Cost)

The price the consumer is willing to pay for the product is equal to the status and appearance of the company plus the cost to make the product and value it provides to the customer.

If you want to raise the value of your product or service quickly, you can make high-quality content that positions you to be perceived as providing a high-value service.

THE BENEFIT OF A BEAUTIFUL BRAND

So if you want to raise the product value to a premium, the equation would look like this:

($1000 premium PV) = (by doubling efforts in brand perception + increasing marketing quality) this multiplies the (cost of product and value it adds)

For a digital product that only cost you $150 to make and it provides realistically $100 of value to the customer, then you could greatly increase the cost of the product by increasing the imagery and wording that represents the product.

PV = (2+2) x (100+150) doubling effort
PV = 4 x 250 quadruples product value
PV = $1000 resulting in higher price

The difference in branding is easy to see at high levels, take a minute an compare the Ritz Carlton logo to Motel 8 and you will see what I mean. Quality branding looks expensive.

- Focus -

"ONLY FOCUS ON INTELLIGENT AND DECISIVE

EFFORTS. THE RESULTING
ACTIONS TURN POTENTIAL
INTO REALITY.
WITHOUT CREATIVE
CONTROL, ARTISTIC IDEAS
CAN RUN WILD."

- SIMON HAWK -

CHAPTER 2

BUILDING A VEHICLE FOR SUCCESS

How to develop the concept in 6 steps :

1. Select what you are going to sell. (This will define your product)

2. Decide who you are going to sell to. (This will define your customer)

3. Choose how you are going to sell it. (This will define which platform is used)

4. Determine how much you are going to sell it for. (This will define the price and value of the product)

5. Estimate how many of them you are going to sell. (This will define the distribution model)

6. Figure out when you are going to sell the products. (This will define your timeline for launching your business)

HOW TO CHOOSE A PRODUCT TO SELL

1. Identify or create products that solve

a problem, save money or make money.

2. Find products you and other people are passionate about.

3. Find products with branding potential or an item you can improve.

4. Research trends actively and act fast.

5. Find products that fulfill guilty pleasures. People buy out of habit.

6. Identify and serve niche segments.

7. Spot business opportunities absolutely everywhere, look around.

8. Focus on a skill you have to sell.

9. Take the information you have Learned here and teach it to someone else.

10. Take a service or product you currently offer and optimize it.

CHOOSE A PRODUCT OR SERVICE TO SELL

Common product to sell online include :

DIGITAL PRODUCTS -
eBooks, eCourses, Affiliate Content,

Audiobooks, Templates, Software, SaaS, Applications & Documents

PHYSICAL PRODUCTS -
Books, Apparel, Electronics, Vitamins, Tea, Coffee, Pets , Health & Fitness Equipment

PHYSICAL SERVICES -
You can earn commission for lead generation for: Roofing, Construction Solar Installation and Gym memberships.

DIGITAL SERVICES -
Coding, Web design, Copywriting, Virtual Assistance, Online Training, Online Teaching, Project Management, Graphics Design, Advertising, Social Media Marketing and consulting
for any industry or niche.

HOW TO BEGIN SELLING ONLINE

After you have selected a product and are ready to go to market there a few steps to take before you begin setting up an online store.

Be sure to have these aspects completed:

- Do market research.
- Finalize products to sell.
- Identify your customer base.
- Segment your audiences.
- Research on what eCommerce platform you'd like to sell on.
- Create high-quality product content.
- Create a strategy to market to your potential customers.

SELECT WHERE TO SELL ONLINE

While there are many options to choose from the options below have the longest history and best reputation.
Each can be used to sell the same product and many people sell on multiple platforms.

AMAZON - is great for selling everything from books to bicycles, you have it made, they sell it and you ship it. (Or send to a fulfillment center)

EBAY - is good for selling items that may have more value to specific buyers and allows auction bidding.

ETSY - is nice for selling homemade goods and crafted items that have a personalized touch or are customized.

SHOPIFY - is great for selling any item and opening a quick online store.

CHOOSING AN ONLINE PLATFORM FOR SALES

Each online platform has its benefits and limitations, so it is important to review the functions needed before selecting. Knowing what your online business needs to be able to do is essential to define which site to use, as each has limitations.

WOOCOMERCE - is the most customizable platform and can be very powerful for selling any service.

INSTAGRAM - is a very good way to sell items by engaging with your following, Instagram stores can connect to Shopify.

FACEBOOK MARKETPLACE - is a very connected platform for showcasing products at a local level.

CRATEJOY - is a good option for subscription box services and converting your one-time sales into recurring purchases. Repackaging items to sell them as a bundle works very well.

CHOOSE A WAY TO DISTRIBUTE

How the customer is going to receive the product or service is very important. Determining how this will happen in advance is essential for choosing how you set up and operate your business. Carefully consider what will be most efficient in the long run.

Dropshipping : Physical product sold online and shipped directly from manufacturer to customer.

Fulfillment Center : Physical product manufactured and provided to the fulfillment center for delivery to customers.

Self-Delivery : Physical products delivered by postage or in person to a physical location.

Digital Delivery : Digital products delivered by e-mail or link to a digital location.

CHOOSE A WAY TO PROFIT

Besides the normal routine of posting a photo of a product for purchase on an online store, there are alternative ways to profit online and sell information :

1:1 Coaching / Consulting / Training - If you have a service or product that is complex or requires training you will want to speak to clients directly to help them overcome obstacles.

1:Many Coaching / Consulting / Training - If you want to deliver information to large groups or corporations, streaming videos and conference calls will be the best way to reach a larger audience.

Affiliate Marketing - Digital & Physical Products like software or memberships can be sold so you don't have to make anything. You just market other products.

Commission - Digital & Physical Product sales like Equipment or subscriptions can be sold for other companies.

DEFINE A DREAM CUSTOMER

At the beginning of the chapter, I highlighted a step about deciding WHO you are going to sell to.

You need to define who is your "Target Customer" or ideal client or dream customer.

This will be the type of person who you love engaging with, purchases the most and is the easiest to work with.

This can be done easily by creating avatars. An avatar is a description of the characteristics of a dream customer.

To create an avatar, make a list of the ideal customer's traits including;
Age, Income, Occupation, Family Type, Personality Type and any affiliations.

Keep in mind you can have multiple avatars for each product, and market specifically to each. Just don't try to market to all avatars at once in one ad.

PICK A THEME

A theme can be related to your brand or to the industry you are selling in.

Often times themes are dominated by male or female demographics.

Strength and automotive influences work well for masculine products. Flexibility and self care are often more prevalent in feminine products.

The theme of your brand should relate directly to your product and provide content that is relatable to customers.

Extreme athletes have been conditioned to like bold neon graphics,
while yoga instructors lean towards

plant based imagery.

Choose a theme that is easy to create initially and you can make content for simply. The more complex the theme the more complicated the graphics.

PLAN IT FIRST

Start this process by coming up with a plan and writing it down.

Make yourself a list of the steps that have not been done yet.

If you are starting from scratch or launching a new company your list will be longer and your plan will require 30 days to complete.

If you are improving a business or rebranding this may be a short list that can be accomplished in several days.

THEN DO IT

Whether you hire someone else or do it yourself, use your plan to go item by item and complete each task.

Start at the top and finish at the bottom. Take it step by step. Day by day. You can do it, I believe in you and am confident you will achieve your goals with a little focus!

- Explore -

" EXPLORE YOUR OPTIONS AND THEN MAKE A DECISION ON WHAT CREATIVE DIRECTION YOU WANT TO GO."

- SIMON HAWK -

CHAPTER 3

BREAK DOWN OF RESOURCES

What you will need on this adventure :

A way to communicate - Working remotely requires constant contact and communication through a variety of channels to manage the business.

A way to create - Each business concept requires creating documents, content and products to sell.

A way to document - For people to understand what you are selling or offering they must be able to see it.

A way to connect - Online businesses require collaboration and the sharing of information. You must be able to connect with others and distribute data to your team or customers.

CANVA

I have been using digital art software since it was conceived, literally.
I grew up with Microsoft paint and a

little turtle that made lines behind it on the very first Macintosh computer.

Canva is one of the simplest design tools I have ever used and provides the easiest access to images and photos.

What used to take me hours to do in adobe I can mock up in minutes on this app from my phone or my laptop.

You can quickly format images for a variety of platforms and work from templates. The logos below were mocked up in Canva to reduce time.

ADOBE CREATIVE SUITE

This is now a digital subscription model which allows you to download the program you need for a monthly fee instead of buying software.

The programs below are all offered in the Adobe Creative Cloud Service :

Photoshop - edit photos by altering the pixels. Great for combining images and creating graphics by painting.

Illustrator - edit vectors by moving points and creating shapes. Great for logos and product design.

Indesign - create documents and edit text for use in publications. Great for creating newsletters and magazines.

Premiere - edit videos and add text. Great for courses or commercials.

Lightroom - edit and retouch photos. Great for batch editing of photography.

LAPTOP

This is the most powerful tool and your virtual office building.

You can make products, request products to be made, build online stores and start online businesses from this single piece of equipment.

For design purposes and because of branding I continually purchase Macbook Pro's for their consistent high-quality. I highly recommend purchasing a newer model Macbook, if you are on a budget, search for refurbished models.

The best era for used is the 2015 models.

Viewing complex information and reading long financial documents is much easier on a larger screen. I prefer the 15" models to the 13" for graphics.

3D software and video editing is best done on a desktop, so this is essential to upgrading your designs or content.

HOT SPOT

Communication is key, a laptop is useless for internet based applications if it cannot connect to a server.

A mobile hotspot is essential for connecting to WiFi while traveling.

Netgear makes a unit I am partial to because of great branding. It is called The Nighthawk LTE Mobile Hotspot is rugged and durable unit perfect for travel. It is the best unit for AT&T.

Other options include :
The Jetpack 8800 is the best for Verizon
The MiFi 8000 is the best for Sprint.
The Inseego 5G MiFi M1000 is the best for Verizon.
The HTC 5G Hub is the best Multipurpose Hub.
The Roaming Man is the best International Hotspot.

SMART PHONE

Your phone is really a handheld super computer that can perform 80% of the functions a laptop can. With this single device you can manage an entire social media agency or operate a consulting agency with nothing else but a smartphone.

There are thousands of options now and the most important factor will always be the storage capacity, battery life, processor speed and camera quality.

Whenever possible invest in the tools.

The sharper the tool the more effective.

For consistent quality and because of branding, I continually purchase Apple products. Which ensures all of my devices sync easily.

The best smartphones of 2020 were : iPhone 7S, XR and on a budget the 6S. Other options are the Samsung Galaxy Note 9 or S10, Pixel 3 or LG V40.

- Invest -

" INVEST IN YOURSELF AND PURCHASE THE TOOLS YOU NEED TO RUN YOUR

BUSINESS REMOTELY. TAKE YOUR ONLINE ENTERPRISE SERIOUSLY AND BUILD A MOBILE OFFICE SO YOU CAN WORK FROM THE BEACH. "

- SIMON HAWK -

CHAPTER 4

PLANNING THE WORK

Outlining what needs done and when is essential to planning projects.
I start each week by analyzing my workload through a BrainDump.

You can start by writing down all the things you need to do and thoughts about how to market products and tasks that build up to your goals.

This strategy can also be used with a new client when you need all the information about a project.

I find it is especially important to make more than just a todo list I try to put out all the concepts surrounding the subject to begin developing a full picture of what can and should be done first.

HOW TO PRIORITIZE TASKS

For keeping everything organized and

prioritized I make lists and take notes on each project or client.

I suggest using : Google Drive for all note taking and sharing files.
Stay organized by grouping subjects like clients in parent folders and resources for each client in subfolders.

I make lists of tasks that need done and then I prioritize my tasks to break down the goals into actionable steps that fall into 3 categories :

A. Urgent - Needs done today
B. Necessary - Done by tomorrow
C. Not essential - Done by end of week

Applying project management tactics to launching a brand can greatly help to quickly complete a long list of tasks.

HOW TO PLAN A TIMELINE

Outlining when important tasks need to

be done by is critical to accomplishing tasks on time.

After creating your priority list of tasks you can space them out over a week, month and 3 month period.

It's great to establish soft and hard deadlines as well.

Soft deadlines allow you to creates rough drafts and get feedback on a project before it is due.

Hard deadlines set a defined time for when all revisions and edits need to be completed by.

You can update your Google Calendar to notify you when they're due with alarms. There are many project management tools for monitoring progress.

WHAT IS KANBAN

The Kanban Method is a process developed in Japan by an industrial engineer at Toyota to improve manufacturing efficiency.

The core principles of the Kanban are :

- Visualize the flow of work
- Limit WIP (Work in Progress)
- Make Process Policies Explicit
- Implement Feedback Loops
- Improve Collaboratively
- Evolve Experimentally

This may sounds complex but it in reality it is simple and looks like this :

HOW TO KANBAN

Kanban can be used to monitor task progress and ensure completion of projects. It is my favorite PM tool!

Step 1 : Divide a whiteboard or paper into three columns.

Label the columns "To Do", "Doing" and "Done."

Step 2 : Add post-it notes or draw squares with 1 task in each box.

Add every small task that needs to occur to complete the bigger project.

Step 3 : As you begin each task move it from "Todo" to "Doing".
This will allow you to visually monitor how many items are in the pipeline.

Step 4 : Once each task is completed, move the box from "Doing" to "Done".

This system enables you to quickly see what is not done and where to focus.

HOW TO GANTT

A Gantt chart allows you to visually plan progress along a timeline.

Similar to Kanban, this strategy uses blocks to represent when things need to be done week to week.

You can edit and download a copy of

the Gantt Chart Template I created with Canva by visiting the link below :
bit.ly/GanttChartSimonHawk

- Waves -

" LIFE AND ALL THINGS COME IN WAVES. THERE WILL BE PRODUCTIVE

TIMES AND TIMES
FOR REST.
PAY ATTENTION TO THESE
WAVES AND WAIT FOR
THE RIGHT TIME TO
CHARGE FORWARD."

- SIMON HAWK -

CHAPTER 5

PROJECT MANAGEMENT + OUTSOURCING

It is important to define who will do what and when, remember if you can't do something well, find someone who can.

If you are not artistic or do not have the time to invest in resources you can outsource the design work.

If you are not a natural writer you can outline the topics you need written and contract a copywriter.

If you are not a web designer you can create a list of pages and features, then hire a developer online.

Outsourcing can be fast, fun, affordable & successful only if the project is managed properly.

Project management tools can be used to delegate tasks to outsourcers.

BUSINESS PLAN OUTLINE

Writing down how you want to build

your business and defining how you will operate that business is all part of your business plan.

It is important to develop this document as it can be referred back to in times of confusion or if questions arise about how things should function.

The plan does not need to be complicated at first and will grow with the business as it changes.

You can include an outline of how your business receives work and completes projects. You can list the types of products you will make and how they will be made. You can plan out who will do the work and how you will communicate with your team.

All of these items will dictate how you get things done from a big picture.

HOW TO SETUP THE PROJECT QUICKLY

This form breaks down the steps to launching a new project, business or brand. Anytime a new goal is set there are steps that are taken to achieve it and they should be organized at the beginning of the project.

Project Outlines can be used to quickly communicate any task and standardize requests for work.

- You can download the form here : bit.ly/BusinessModelOutline

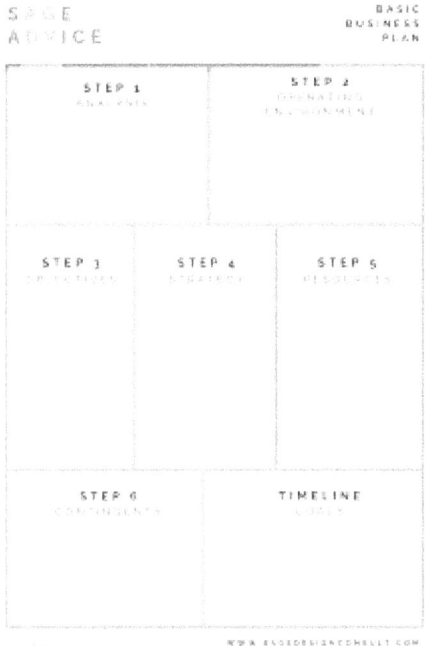

HOW TO MANAGE REMOTE WORKERS

Asking someone to help you with a project places the burden and responsibility on that person.

To make their job easier and properly manage remote workers I suggest you:

1. Outline the project tasks in a

SCOPE OF WORK document.

2. List the tasks in order of priority & indicate priorities with COLORS.

3. Set a specific BUDGET for how much each task is worth.

4. Set a SOFT DEADLINE for reviewing & a HARD DEADLINE for completion.

5. Provide all the IMAGE CONTENT & COPY of TEXT in an organized file.

6. COMMUNICATE actively & provide positive FEEDBACK in the process.

SCOPE OF WORK

The best way to organize tasks and request work from overseas teams is to complete a Scope of Work form before sending a payment.

You can download this form here : bit.ly/scopeofworksage

This form breaks down the tasks and

the expectations for deliveries as well as gathers valuable information about the project to help manage the prioritization of work.

SCOPE OF WORK
SAGE ADVICE

PROJECT OBJECTIVES | SCHEDULE & MILESTONES
INDIVIDUAL TASKS | DELIVERABLES
PAYMENT INFORMATION | EXPECTED OUTCOMES
TERMS, CONDITIONS & REQUIREMENTS

DESIGN BY SIMON HAWK — WWW.SAGEDESIGNCONSULT.COM

BUDGETING

Outlining when things need to be done by and monitoring progress with charts. There are two main factors to budget when launching a brand or managing a project.

TIME - Every task takes a certain amount of time to complete and you must budget your time according to your priority list or timeline for the project.

Where you invest your time should be according to a plan if you are to meet deadlines and complete jobs on time.

MONEY - Each task costs different values and depending on the amount of money available, it is critical to stick to a budget.

Where you invest your money should be in the items that are most important, due soon or cannot be done by yourself.

HOW TO ORGANIZE A PROJECT ONLINE

I organize my projects using online systems that allow me to share documents, timelines and resources with my team members.

For delegation of work and organization I suggest using : **www.airtable.com**

Many other people prefer : www.Clickup.com

www.Asana.com
www.Trello.com

These will help you assign steps and communicate with your team remotely.

Sharing responsibilities and clearly defining what needs done is essential to successful remote work.

Always set up a task list and verify it with your team before passing it off.

- Success -

"THE ONES WHO SUCCEED IN THIS WORLD ARE THE ONES WHO GET UP AND SEEK OPPORTUNITIES TO IMPROVE PROCESSES, ORGANIZE INFORMATION,

AND HELP OTHERS.
IF YOU CAN'T FIND AN
OPPORTUNITY, MAKE ONE
FOR YOURSELF."
- SIMON HAWK -

CHAPTER 6

BRAND DESIGN OPTIMIZATION

Whether you are launching a new business or improving an existing one, customizing your brand is an ongoing progress.

These are 6 things you will need to improve to set sail quickly :

1. Get a high quality logo/icon and custom font designed for your brand.
2. Get professional photos of yourself, your staff, your services and products.
3. Get a customized website with a store or upload a new logo and photos.
4. Get a Facebook page and group for the business or update with new content.
5. Get a customized Facebook cover photo designed or update your current image.
6. Get all other social media profiles to include the same high quality imagery that focuses on your service/product.

LOGO DESIGN

My personal style for logo design is carefully calculated and crafted with attention to detail that requires getting to know the brand intimately.

I personally suggest researching your target customers and the market to find a strong design direction that will elevate the brand. Search for an image or shape that represents the core of the company and pair it with a font that accentuates it.

I believe you can capture a companies essence and translate it into an effective icon through art, which often takes time. It can be done easily by drawing basic outlines and sketching concepts on paper to give to a designer.

Ultimately, it needs to be a memorable mark that represents the company. The simpler it is and the more balanced/symmetrical it is, the better!

PICK A COLOR PALETTE

Colors within design are used to communicate emotions and add character to simple shapes.

You can use a "color psychology wheel" to select the type of emotional responses you want your logo to have.

Depending on your market and the nature of your business you want to select a range of tones from light to dark to use for fonts, backgrounds and accents on your website.

Choosing colors and sticking to them is important for continuity of branding. It keeps content looking unified as well.

A palette can be sampled from a photo or a piece of artwork by choosing 3-6 colors and saving them in a style guide.

A style guide is a document where you can refer back to the color palette, logo and font type.

PICK A CUSTOM FONT

The fonts you choose are as important as the words you choose to write.

A great font is customized to the

brand and further drives home the message of the logo. Go to www.1001freefonts.com/ for free fonts.

If your company deals with a very sophisticated clientele and needs to express professionalism, then a font with Serifs is recommended.

If you are a more modern company or have a younger customer, Sans Serif fonts are perfectly acceptable.

As a general rule of thumb, it is rare to use more than 2 fonts within a brand. A large wide font can be used for headlines, signs and advertisements. A thinner, short font can be used for the majority of the content. The most critical factor is that it is easy to read and. Recognize from far away and at a small scale.

SELECT A DESIGN STYLE & THEME

The style of your design is often dictated by the market you are in.

For example men's athletic equipment often has a militaristic design & style to the advertising, because that is what those types of clients have responded well to.

Deciding on a style & theme can be targeted towards a certain type of customer as well.

If you are selling services to people who own boats, it would make sense to select a nautical style or a theme inspired by the ocean.

Themes can be planned by creating mood boards using www.Pinterest.com or you can collect images in a Google document that represent the style that you want to create in your content. Creating reference guide will help you stay consistent.

NO BUDGET CANVA

If you have no budget for logo design or branding that's ok! With $0 to spend You will just have to get creative and DIY. (If you want it done Do-It-Yourself) Roll up your sleeves and put on your creative thinking cap to tackle this task by yourself.

Here are few tips to get you started :

USE CANVA -

If you don't feel creative, find a logo design template you like and don't change the layout much as a designer already properly placed the elements and selected shapes that work.

USE THE FREE RESOURCES OF THE INTERNET! -
If you don't feel inspired, find design inspiration on blogs or, look for design cues from the market you are in to create something that is unique from the competition.

SMALL BUDGET ADOBE CREATIVE

If you have a low budget of anywhere from $50 to $100 to spend you can get better quality images and more customization to your branding.

Adobe Creative Suite offers Photoshop, Illustrator, Lightroom, Indesign and Premiere. For a low monthly fee you can get online access to these powerful programs.

Here are few tips to get you started :

USE ILLUSTRATOR TO BUILD DESIGNS ON A GRID AND KEEP IT BALANCED!

(This allows you to place points on a grid and build logos that are perfectly aligned or follow the golden rule)

USE PHOTOSHOP TO ADD DEPTH!

(Designs can look flat without layers, this allows you to add layers of texture and different effects like painting with a brush to make content pop)

MEDIUM BUDGET UPWORK & FIVERR

If you have a reasonable budget of anywhere from $100 to $500 to invest, you can pay for even better quality images. Allowing a freelancer to customize your concept will elevate your branding if done correctly.

www.Upwork.com is an excellent platform for posting design jobs and hiring freelancers. There are many designers from other countries with different styles and backgrounds.

www.Fiverr.com is another option which allows for more localized freelancers and even designers you can meet with in person depending on your city.

Here is a tip to insure the best results :

INTERVIEW 3 FREELANCERS PER JOB
If you want to get a accurate estimate on the cost and design options, request a sample of their work to compare results.

LARGE BUDGET DESIGN AGENCY

If you have a relatively high budget of anywhere from $1000 to $5000 to spend, you can request premium quality content and receive high levels of customization to your branding.

Small boutique agencies like www.SageDesignConsult.com focus on a Lead Designer spearheading the operation, to working closely with you, to define a specific direction and create a unified vision.

Large agencies allow you to access a team of designers and receive many

different options, often relying on
outsourcing and heavy communication
to finalize a good graphic.

Here is a tip to help you find a good fit :

HIRE AN AGENCY YOU LOVE TO WORK WITH

If you see their work and love it,
request a quote for a similar style.

- Style -

" WHEN IT COMES TO STYLE
YOU GET WHAT
YOU PAY FOR.

DON'T EXPECT
INTELLIGENT AND
INSPIRED DESIGNS
OR WORK FOR CHEAP"

- SIMON HAWK -

CHAPTER 7

WEBSITE SETUP & FUNNEL UPGRADE

A website can be set up to be much more than a portfolio. Think of your website as an employee, a digital storefront, a salesperson, a mailbox and a news channel just for your business.

When upgrading a website, think about how you want this space they enter to serve or direct them as a customer. I tell my web design clients, the comparison between a good website and a bad site is the same as a clothing store.

When you walk into a used clothing store, no one helps you shop and it's cheap. When you walk into a designer store like Armani, you are greeted at the door, they suggest upsells and they offer for you to join their exclusive club upon checkout. Your website can do these same things.

THEME & COLOR

Start your online business by opening

a digital storefront with style.
Select a theme that is inline with your market and your target demographic.

If it is a masculine athletic product, select dark colors and accent with red or neons. Themes for workout equipment are usually military, rough terrain, metal, modern and futuristic.

If it is a feminine natural health service, select light colors and accent with green or soft blue hues. Themes for health products are usually ocean, florals, plants, minimal and watercolor.

The theme and color of your website should enhance the message of the company or create a vibe that aligned with your brand.

Stick to a simple theme and choose 3-4 colors to use continually for brand consistency across all platforms.

BASIC WEB DESIGN

Portfolios and artists looking to display their work can easily use www.wix.com as a beginner. It is very easy to learn, though.

The site has limitations for developing advanced features and accepting payments in certain countries.

This platform is best used for fast, affordable portfolios that need to be created on a low budget or transferred to a client with little web experience.

The sites below are examples of Wix premium sites I have developed with advanced features like online services and appointment scheduling.

PRO WEBDESIGN

Serious service providers and businesses looking to fully customize their website continually suggest using www.wordpress.com as a professional.

Wordpress themes enable you to quickly apply templates and tools to build even faster websites.

The theme www.elementor.com is widely recognized as one of the best options. It allows for drag and drop customization for intermediate web designers. Many tutorials exist for it.

This platform is best used for fully customizable sites that will include automation integration from other platforms. It provides the most options for developers and coders to add elements to your site. It has the advantage of being a free platform to start and is by far the most versatile platform for multiple markets.

ECOMMERCE WEB DESIGN
SHOPIFY & WOOCOMERCE

If you care more about selling products than creating fancy designs, then **www.shopify.com** is a great option for an eCommerce businesses.

Shopify is really easy to use and is widely accepted by beginner drop shippers and small clothing stores. It allows you to upload a catalog or line of products and begin selling quickly.

Another similar option is :
www.woocomerce.com
WooCommerce is as powerful as Shopify, and it gives you even more control since you can decide where you want to host your online store, but it's by far less beginner-friendly, and certain features aren't included in the core system. Their monthly subscription cost is very reasonable.

SALES FOCUSED DESIGN & CLICKFUNNELS

If you want to learn more about marketing and selling products online, then **www.clickfunnels.com** has a very good training program called the

One Funnel Away Challenge to explain how to sell more products online.

It provides a lot of tools to help people easily build sales focused websites. If you don't like writing, they offer a service that generates copy for you easily at www.funnelscripts.com

The sites below show a simple funnel used to market an eBook.

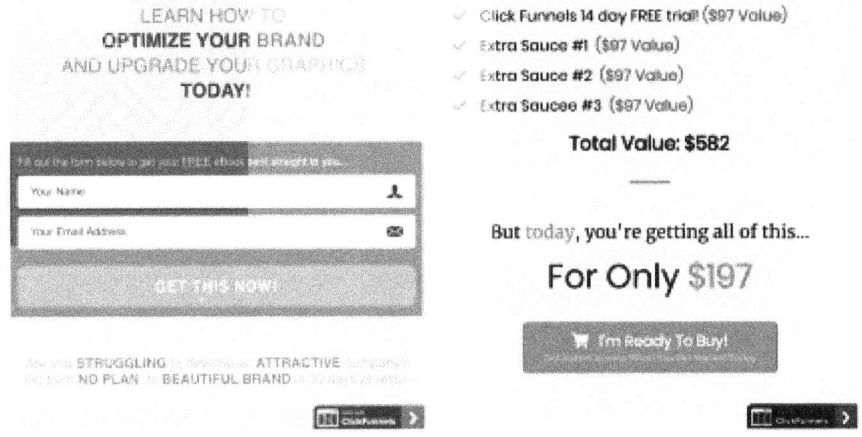

DOMAIN HOSTING

You will need to purchase and host your domain to launch your website.
I personally suggest using
www.godaddy.com
www.BlueHost.com
www.Nameserver.net

If you are going to purchase multiple websites it is best to keep them all under one roof. This will help you to make access the settings to make changes and update payment for domain renewals from one singular point.

Maintaining control of your domains is important and I do not suggest allowing agencies or freelancers to purchase domains on your behalf. Always secure and protect your Intellectual Property! Placing your sensitive data on a protected or dedicated server is the best way to Keep IP safe!

www.liquidweb.com
www.a2hosting.com

EMAIL AUTOMATION

Automating your emails helps improve the relevancy and timeliness of your campaigns. You can use triggers and workflows to automatically send messages to consumers after they take a specific action like subscribing or purchasing.

To automate your email marketing you can use www.activecampaign.com

ActiveCampaign has all the features of a premium service , but the low price and easy set up is great for beginners.
In a few steps, you can provision a marketing automation platform.

For Large databases and high sending volumes it is not the ideal option.

A few alternatives are :
www.getresponse.com
www.zohocampaigns.com
www.mailchimp.com

BUSINESS AUTOMATION

There are many wonderful tools for automating business and productivity tasks which give you more free time.

I highly recommend www.zapier.com Zapier is an online automation tool that connects your favorite apps, such as Gmail, Slack, Mailchimp, and more.

It allows You to connect two or more apps to automate repetitive tasks without coding or relying on developers to build the integration.

An alternative for equally reliable automation is www.IFTTT.com

IFITTT is a freeware web-based service that creates chains of simple conditional statements, called applets.

An applet is triggered by changes that occur within other web services such as Gmail, Facebook, Telegram, Instagram, or Pinterest.

- Speed -

"THE FASTER YOU CAN LAUNCH A SITE OR PRODUCT AND GET FEEDBACK, THE BETTER . LET A FOCUS GROUP OR TEST MARKET REACT TO A DESIGN QUICKLY AND ADAPT IT"
- SIMON HAWK -

CHAPTER 8

ADVERTISING & DESIGN

These 9 strategies for developing beautiful ads will allow you to quickly and easily advertise your brand :

1. Create Eye Catching Images
2. Write Engaging Copy
3. Select Relevant Demographics
4. Use Facebook and Instagram ad creator to help you use your content
5. Take your most viewed Facebook Video and run it as a Youtube Ad
6. Take the description of your business and run it as a Google Ad
7. Make sure to install your Facebook Pixel and setup Google Analytic
8. Hire a freelancer to help design the ad
9. Hire an agency to manage the project

Driving traffic to your site and offering your services to as many people as possible is next. Prepare for traffic by testing your site's links and functions.

CREATE EYE CATCHING IMAGES

The image is often the hook of an advertisement. It must grab the viewers attention or stop them from scrolling past your post.

It is important to use imagery that catches the attention of your target audience and speaks directly to them.

If your focus is on action sports and you create an ad that is boring, it may not get as many reactions as a depiction of someone being extreme.

Here are a few ways to get people to respond to your content :
• Create images which Immediately create a positive emotional feeling.
• Build an emotional roller coaster using a slide show, walk through a journey or experience.
• Surprise them, but don't shock them. Show incredible before and after images.

WRITE ENGAGING COPY THAT SELLS

Writing to encourage readers to react, comment or click on something requires a few different strategies.

First and foremost you need a purpose or a goal to direct your writing.

Clearly define the following aspects of the advertisement to outline your pitch :
• What you want to say?
• Who do you want to say it to?
• How do you want them to react?
• What do you want them to do?
• When you want them to do it?
• List the keywords of your product.

Once you have established these factors, create an ad that :

• Catches their attention in the first sentence with an emotional trigger
• Tells a story or describes the product in a way that takes them from point A to B
• Concludes with a call to action or offer

SELECT RELEVANT DEMOGRAPHICS

The goal of targeted advertisements is to show your product to only people who would be potential customers.

If you are selling an educational product for college students in the

United States, you do not need to show that ad to elderly people or anyone outside of the US.

Selecting the relevant demographics for your advertisement is important to maximize the effect on your ad spend.

Wasting money on promoting a service to someone who cannot access it is inefficient and avoidable by targeting only relevant demographics.

You can define who you want to advertise to by creating a Customer Avatar describing your ideal client.

Run ads targeted to the avatars demographics and characteristics.

USE FACEBOOK ADS & INSTAGRAM ADS

Facebook and Instagram are an ideal place to promote products and advertise services easily. Any Facebook post or video can be submitted as an ad for approval. The ad creator platform is an excellent tool for creating slideshows from old content.

There are many factors for why ads do not get approved, most of them revolve around music copyright issues, controversial content or misleading copy. To ensure your ads are approved regularly review the ad guidelines for both platforms to understand what you can and cannot use as an ad.

As a general rule of thumb you want to use high quality resolution content that is bright or has high contrast to be easy to read on mobile devices.

Ads should disrupt the users feed as they scroll and give them a reason to click or continue watching.

RUN YOUR BEST POSTS AS YOUTUBE ADS

"Multiplying your content" is a great concept for taking videos you have already made and reposting them.

By sampling from a longer video or remixing video footage you already posted, you can multiply your content.

If you have a video that shows your product or service, that has gotten really great comments and high engagement, then you already know that it is good content.

You can take that content and run it as a Youtube ad by editing the video with text or voiceover a new message.

Low budget advertisements can be just as effective if the content is relevant to the viewer.

A well filmed home video or authentic conversation about your offer turned into a Youtube ad can be more relatable than a traditional infomercial.

RUN YOUR BIZ DESCRIPTION AS A GOOGLE AD

Google AdWords increases leads and customers by allowing your web address, a short description to be ranked on Google's search engine.

Google is where people go to ask questions, so this is where you insert yourself as an answer to a problem.

If your campaigns are set up properly, it

has the potential to send extremely targeted leads to your website, E-commerce website, opt-in form or other online property.

You can visit www.ads.google.com to run pay per clicks or impressions and have your link featured on the first page of Google results by outbidding your keyword competitors.

An important part of this process is monitoring results and improving the copy of the ad to increase conversions.

SETUP ANALYTICS & INSTALL PIXELS

To fully understand the data behind your ad you need to install Facebook Pixel and Google Analytics. This will allow you to see the following :
• Where your traffic is coming from.
• Who is seeing your ad.
• Where they go after they click on it.

Facebook pixels in enables :
• Ad Retargeting to show people who watched your ad and, another follow-up ad
• Creating Lookalike audiences that

share similarities and are likely to buy.
www.facebook.com/business/learn/face
Book-ads-pixel

Google Analytics specifically helps :
• Compare online campaigns and traffic from multiple sources.
• Track bounce rate from website.
• Identify worst performing pages.
• Visually displays what countries your visitors are coming from. www.analytics.google.com

HIRE A FREELANCER TO DESIGN IT

If you have other things to focus on, like building the products or running the company, you may want to consider hiring a freelancer to help you with advertising.

If you have a small to medium budget of anywhere from $100 to $500 to spend monthly for advertising, you can pay for a virtual assistant or hire a contractor to manage the campaigns.

Allowing someone to assist you with advertising may greatly improve the campaign results by avoiding any learning curves or technical mistakes.

www.Upwork.com is an excellent platform for hiring / posting ad content creators and campaign managers to run ads for you.

www.Fiverr.com is another alternative for finding PPC ad creators and managers at a local level.

HIRE AN AGENCY TO MANAGE IT

If you want the best results from a large campaign and want multiple people attending to your project, hire an agency to manage the whole thing.

If you have a large budget, anything over $1,000 a month in ad spend, you can pay for a team of advertising professionals to focus their skills on your campaign.

Allowing an agency to manage the project will give you access to all their experience and resources to increase / improve conversions.

The key to finding a good agency is

selecting one with experience in your field or market.

The ability to connect with your ideal customers and the background knowledge from the industry will allow them to create content easily and write more effectively.

- Perfection -

" BEWARE THE SEARCH FOR PERFECTION, AS IT IS AN ENDLESS JOURNEY. A DESIGN ACHIEVES NEAR PERFECTION, NOT WHEN THERE IS NOTHING LEFT TO ADD, BUT WHEN THERE IS NOTHING LEFT TO REMOVE. IF EVERY ELEMENT IS

ESSENTIAL, IT IS PERFECT."
- SIMON HAWK -

CHAPTER 9

LAUNCHING THE BOAT

& PROMOTING YOUR BRAND

After you have developed your product, written offers, built your site and placed ads, there is still work to do.

It is not all smooth sailing ahead. Without a proper launch, a strong engine and regular maintenance, you won't move forward.

This chapter is about plotting the course to success, gaining speed and maintaining momentum for growth.

Proper planning and preparing for the future is essential to long term success.

On a long journey, you do not want to burn all your fuel at once or be without a Plan B, in case something breaks.

STRATEGY LAYOUT

To launch your business, you need to

plot the course first.

Make a list of the following :
• Where you want your business to go
(Fortune 500 or leader of local area)

• When you want to accomplish this growth by
(Grow to 50 employees by 2025)

• What you will need to do to get there
(List the steps to prepare for launch)

• How you are going to get there
(List the things that need to happen)

• Who is going to help you get there
(List the people or companies needed)

Then come up with a "Plan B".
An alternative in case you have to pivot and anticipate X factors like funding falling through.
• Always have a plan B considered
• Always have an exit Strategy
• Always focus on success not failure
* Successful people know things go wrong.

30 DAY PLAN COMMIT & ANALYZE

Once you have established a strategy, you need to select a starting day, and commit to it. Deciding to take action and dedicating yourself to a schedule will give you a time frame, as well as a list of daily tasks to accomplish.

Committing to a 30 day plan will allow you to focus your time and energy to completing tasks. It will also give you an end date at which time you can analyze your performance.

Analyzing performance is as important as commitment;, you do not want to commit to taking the wrong actions.

Once you complete a month of habit-forming tasks, review what you have accomplished and determine what areas you need assistance with, and what areas you excel at.

Do more of what you are good at, then delegate out what you are less efficient at.

MARKETING BUDGETS

A very simple way to establish a budget for marketing is to make it proportional to the value of your product.

If you have a high-ticket sales item that is worth thousands of dollars in profit, then your budget for marketing can be thousands of dollars a month.

If you have a low volume of sales, and each sales brings in a few hundred dollars, you would want to budget a couple hundred dollars a month for marketing.

According to the Small Business Administration, it is recommended that you spend 7 - 8% percent of your gross revenue on marketing and advertising, if your net profit margin (after all expenses) is in the 10 - 12% percent range.

THE GOAL & KPI

The goal is a point which you aim for. A business goal describes what a company expects to accomplish over a specific period of time.

KPIs are Key Performance Indicators. Points of reference and measurement for achieving goals. These can be used to demonstrate how effectively the company is achieving a business goal.

High-level KPIs may focus on the overall performance of the business, while low-level KPIs can account for increases in followers, sales, leads generated or traffic volume to a website.

Use overarching goals and specific KPIs to make lists of what you want to achieve. Write down how much growth you want to achieve and when you want it to happen by.

SOCIAL MEDIA LIVES & GROUPS

Social media has the power to connect you to consumers and allows you to promote your services directly.

To continually gain new customers and engage your followers, you can provide a behind the scenes look at your operations with the Live features on Facebook and Instagram.

"Going "Live" is a unique opportunity to

show your potential customers what you do and how you do it.

This unedited style of promoting your business is more personal and engages people to speak directly to you, or ask questions that come to your DMs.

Joining Facebook groups about your industry or profession is an excellent way to stay connected and make new connections. Actively posting results or questions will help gain new fans.

CLOSING IN DM'S

After you begin connecting with groups and people on social media, you will have direct messages coming to you asking about your services, rates and requesting information about your business.

This is the perfect opportunity to start practicing closing sales in DMs. Much like speaking directly to a potential client, you want to direct your messages on social media to close a sale.

The goal is of messaging a potential client in DMs should be to :

• Answer questions from the client to build a rapport.
• Provide value by offering solutions to the problems around their question.
• Send them links to social proof or references that you can help them.
• Receive information on how to follow up with a sales call.

BLOGS

Writing your own articles is an excellent way to self-publish information about your service or product. Blogs that include your company name, product name, customer description and industry topics are highly ranked.

A common practice for Search Engine Optimization ranking is creating backlinks, which are articles that refer back to your product or service from another blog. Collaborate with a blog to get featured and backlink to your site.

Writing detailed reviews and

blog posts explaining the benefits of your
business distributed across the internet
will pop up and drive traffic to
your website from people searching for
information on that topic.

Write a short post that answers a
commonly asked question in a new way
or make thought-provoking observations about the industry in a thought-provoking way to
create viral content that can be shared.

PODCAST

People respond really well to
inspirational advice or storytelling
from people in their specific industry.

Actively searching for podcasts and
inquiring about discussing relevant
topics is an excellent way to get
recognized in your field.

Audio is a very powerful tool that can
be used by those who don't like to be
on camera or don't enjoy writing.
If you can talk for hours about a
subject relating to your market, you
can set up your own podcast!

To host your own podcast you need :
• A good microphone

Movo VXR10 or Blue Yeti
• A podcast platform
Soundcloud or Podbean or BuzzSprout
• A podcast cover image
Edit images on Snapseed or Spark Post

EMAIL LIST

It is vital to your long term success with an online business to continually develop your email list.

Your email list should be treated as a valuable asset, and is ultimately is one of your most profitable pieces of intellectual property.

An email list is how you will promote new products and stay connected with clients, encouraging recurring sales. Every new service or opportunity that you offer can instantly be sent to your entire list of clients, which makes it a very powerful tool.

The main goal of advertising is to either sell a product or generate leads. All leads generated leads should be added to your email list. Use automation for this.

Continue to create places on your site and social media for people to enter their email as an ongoing strategy.

- Clarity -

" ONE OF THE EASIEST AND MOST EFFECTIVE STRATEGIES IS TO BE CLEAR. IN DESIGN, IN COPY, IN ADVERTISING AND MARKETING, YOU WANT TO BE CLEAR ABOUT YOUR MESSAGE. BE CRYSTAL CLEAR ABOUT THE BENEFITS OF YOUR PRODUCT OR SERVICE."

- SIMON HAWK -

THE JOURNEY

¡Felicidades! You've made it to the end and now you know how to launch a business from a boat.

This chapter serves as a closure to the story of how to launch a business from a boat. Next, I will review with you the reasons why you should start today. You should commit to your online business, to help you I will provide a few checklists for achieving your goals.

The most important take-away is for you to understand that it is possible to build a strong and beautiful brand easily.

Remember to collaborate with others and ask for help when you reach a point that stumps you. You can't do it all. It is important to enjoy the journey while staying focused on the destination.

Ask your friends for input on design, and

make something that makes you smile.

The business will blossom if you do what you are passionate about.

REVIEW OF THE RESOURCES NEEDED

To set up a mobile office anywhere get :

- Laptop
- Smart Phone
- External Hard Drive
- Mobile WiFi Hotspot

To upgrade the quality of content get :

- DSLR or Mirrorless Drone
- Drone with 1080P or 4k
- Microphone with Noise cancelling
- Gimbal for phone or camera
- Portable LED Light Kit

If you want to stay organized and use project management methods like Kanban in your office you can get :

- Whiteboards
- Dry-erase markers
- Post-it notes
- Note/sketchbooks
- Nice pens & pencils

REVIEW OF HOW TO PRIORITIZE IT ALL

Start each week by analyzing your workload through a BrainDump.

You can start by writing down all the things you need to do, and thoughts about how to market and tasks that build up to your goals.

Use Google Drive for all note-taking and sharing of files that need to be saved.

Break down the goals into actionable steps that fall into 3 categories :

A. Urgent - needs to be done today
B. Necessary - can wait to tomorrow
C. Not essential - done by end of week

For delegation of work and organization I suggest using : Airtable Many other people prefer : Clickup, Asana or Trello

These will help you assign steps and communicate with your team remotely. Sharing responsibilities and clearly defining tasks is key to remote work.

REVIEW OF HOW TO MANAGE IT ALL

For direct communication with clients, employees and customers I suggest setting up a good system for video conferencing and keeping messages organized as well as backed up.

Texting is not a good way to send messages about projects as information needs to be searchable for cross-referencing.

- Use Gmail for email
- Use Grammarly for spell checking
- Use Slack for group messaging
- Use Zoom or Hangouts for video conferencing and screen sharing
- Use the site Calendly for booking appointments

To be honest, speaking directly to employees and keeping group meetings short is the ideal way to motivate staff.

A standup meeting is a great tool to use. Lead a 15 min. overviews of priorities with staff at the beginning of the day to boost productivity.

REVIEW OF HOW TO DESIGN IT ALL

Use Canva to develop simple graphics, use templates, store all your work online and collaborate with a team.

Use Adobe Creative Cloud to design complex graphics and edit high-resolution photos on your computer.

For video editing on your phone use the app VideoLeap or Quik.

For editing photos on your phone use the app SnapSeed or Lightroom.

Use the 3 golden rules for design to keep your brand consistent:

1. Keep It Stupid Simple Stupid - KISS it!
2. Keep it Easy - Make text easy to read!
3. Keep it Classy - Make it timeless!

REVIEW OF HOW TO TRACK IT ALL

For creating proposals, sending invoices, and tracking clients' progress on the fly, develop a repeatable format or template.

Writing new proposals from scratch can be very time consuming and produce inconsistent results for accounting. Without a good template system for efficiency.

You can use the site Proposify to write and track proposals.

You can use PipeDrive to manage your pipeline of sales.

I encourage you to use HubSpot for your CRM system (Customer Relationship Management).

I suggest you try using Joist for simple invoices on the fly.

I recommend using the app Helios for time tracking.

REVIEW OF HOW TO GET PAID & MANAGE IT ALL

Your financial organization system can be improved so that you can receive money easily and the transactions are recorded automatically.

Use QuickBooks for your accounting and submitting invoices.

Use PayPal , Venmo and Stripe for receiving small payments.

Use merchant terminal services like FattMerchant or PayLine for eCommerce and large transactions.

Use Mint and CreditKarma for financial advice and account monitoring.

Always enlist a trusted financial advisor and consult an attorney when purchasing assets or signing contracts of value over $20,000.

AFTERTHOUGHT

I want you to imagine if you were stuck on a boat and needed to launch a new product or start offering a new service from the middle of the water.

Could you do it with your current business model?

What I hope this book has provided to you with are the tools to be able to launch from a boat. I designed the lists of resources you will need on your journey and guides on how to do it step by step to give you direction.

I have worked from a boat and continue to manage my business using these tools from all over the Caribbean. I know that with a phone, a laptop, wifi and focus, you can too.

I believe in you and wish you well on your journey.
If you need help… Send me a SOS!

TeachConsultPR@Gmail.com

- The End -

" THANK YOU FOR READING, I SINCERELY HOPE YOU GAINED KNOWLEDGE FROM THESE PAGES AND THE IDEAS HAVE INSPIRED YOU.

I BELIEVE IN YOU!"

SIMON HAWK

FOR MORE INSPIRATION AND MOTIVATION FOR SUCCESS IN BUSINESS FOLLOW ME ON INSTAGRAM @SIMONHAWK

WWW.INSTAGRAM.COM/ SIMONHAWK

If this book ends up impacting your life please message me to tell me about your experience.

It is my goal to continually offer you support and encourage your growth.

We all need a support network and group of like minded peers to help lift us up.

To join my group on Facebook and connect with other readers of this book :

https://www.facebook.com/groups/Brand.Optimization.Business.Accelerator

https://www.facebook.com/groups/exito.crew

www.ingramcontent.com/pod-product-compliance
Lightning Source LLC
Chambersburg PA
CBHW071621040426
42452CB00009B/1429